SEPTEMBER 11

a testimony

ISBN 0-13-044974-1

SEPTEMBER 11

a testimony

REUTERS

Published by **Pearson Education**

New York • London • San Francisco • Toronto • Sydney • Tokyo • Singapore
Hong Kong • Cape Town • Madrid • Amsterdam • Munich • Paris • Milan

Library of Congress Cataloging-in-Publication Data

A CIP catalog record for this book can be obtained from the Library of Congress

Publisher: Tim Moore
Executive editor: Jim Boyd
Production supervisor: Patti Guerrieri
Marketing manager: Bryan Gambrel
Manufacturing manager: Maura Zaldivar
Editorial assistant: Allyson Kloss
Cover design director: Jerry Votta
Cover designer: Anthony Gemmellaro
Art director: Gail Cocker-Bogusz
Interior design and layout: Meg Van Arsdale

Reuters: Stephen Jukes
Acquisitions editor, Pearson Education, UK: Martin Drewe
Cover art photographer: Ray Stubblebine
Cover photo copyright © 2001 Reuters

In compiling this book, thanks go to many people. At Reuters: Nancy Bobrowitz, Steve Crisp, Izabel Grindal, Elaine Herlihy, Gary Hershorn, Steve Jukes, Peter Morgan, Peter Millership, Paul Mylrea, Jessica Persson, Alexia Singh, Irina Stocker and David Viggers. At Pearson Education: Hannah Cottrill, Helena Dahlstrom, Martin Drewe, Susan Drummond, Peter Marshall, Ian Roberts and Richard Stagg. At Pearson Plc: Rebecca Seymour.

© 2002 by Reuters
Published by Prentice Hall PTR
Prentice-Hall, Inc.
Upper Saddle River, NJ 07458

Prentice Hall books are widely used by corporations and government agencies for training, marketing, and resale.

The publisher offers discounts on this book when ordered in bulk quantities. For more information, contact: Corporate Sales Department, Phone: 800-382-3419; Fax: 201-236-7141; E-mail: corpsales@prenhall.com; or write: Prentice Hall PTR, Corp. Sales Dept., One Lake Street, Upper Saddle River, NJ 07458.

Printed in the United States of America

10 9 8 7 6 5 4 3 2

ISBN 0-13-044974-1

Pearson Education LTD.
Pearson Education Australia PTY, Limited
Pearson Education Singapore, Pte. Ltd.
Pearson Education North Asia Ltd.
Pearson Education Canada, Ltd.
Pearson Educación de Mexico, S.A. de C.V.
Pearson Education—Japan
Pearson Education Malaysia, Pte. Ltd.

We dedicate this book to our six colleagues
from the Reuters family that we lost at the World Trade Center.

It contains a collection of harrowing images that capture the
destruction of September 11, 2001, but that also reflect acts of
great heroism and compassion and the resilience of the human spirit.

It also shows the exceptional work and talent of Reuters photographers.

Tom Glocer
CEO
Reuters

These remarkable pictures record the events of September 11th in a way
that words cannot. They reveal the horrors and they exalt the heroes. They
remind us that we are all involved in this tragedy and that the resilient
spirit and the common purpose we saw on that day are the qualities that
will see us through.

We're proud to be publishing this book
with Reuters to honour those whose lives were lost
and those who fought to save lives.

Marjorie Scardino
Chief Executive
Pearson Plc

At 8:47 a.m. on September 11, 2001, American Airlines Flight 11 slams into the north tower of Manhattan's World Trade Center. Sixteen minutes later, United Airlines Flight 175 plows into the south tower, exploding upon impact. Workers are desperately trying to escape and rescuers are rushing to their aid, when the two towers of the World Trade Center—one of the most imposing symbols of U.S. prosperity—collapse. Thousands of people are buried in the wreckage of the buildings, which were brought down by suicide hijackers at the controls of the two fuel-laden Boeing 767 airliners. Blamed by the U.S. government on Saudi-born Osama bin Laden and his al Qaeda network, the attacks bring comparisons with the December 7, 1941, Japanese assault on Pearl Harbor that left more than 2,300 dead and thrust America into World War II. In the next hour, a third hijacked plane—American Airlines Flight 77, a Boeing 757—is flown into the Pentagon defense headquarters near Washington, D.C.; and a fourth plane—United Airlines Flight 93, a Boeing 757—crashes into a field in Pennsylvania after passengers rush the hijackers.

SEPTEMBER 11

a testimony

Mike Segar

Sean Adair

Sean Adair

Sean Adair

(far left) Hijacked United Airlines Flight 175 flies toward the World Trade Center south tower just seconds before slamming into it at 9:03 a.m. September 11, 2001. The north tower burns after being struck at 8:47 a.m. by American Airlines Flight 11. (middle) Flight 175 explodes upon impact as it plows into the south tower. (right) Seconds later, the south tower is engulfed by flames.

Sean Adair

Sean Adair

Sean Adair

(far left) Black smoke billows from the damaged north tower as the south tower continues to burn. (middle) Glass and rubble spill from the building in the seconds after impact. (right) The north tower weakens in the immediate aftermath of the coordinated attack.

Flight 175 explodes on impact with the south tower of the World Trade Center at 9:03 a.m. as the north tower burns. The Brooklyn Bridge is in the foreground. Television cameras filming the aftermath of the first attack broadcast the second attack live to a stunned nation.

Sara K. Schwittek

People standing on a nearby street point in disbelief at the destruction taking place before their eyes.

Richard Cohen

The twin towers of the World Trade Center pour plumes of black smoke into the sky, casting a shadow over New York City.

Brad Rickerby

People hang out of windows as the north tower of the World Trade Center burns. Rescue workers are powerless to save them. Shortly afterwards, the tower collapsed.

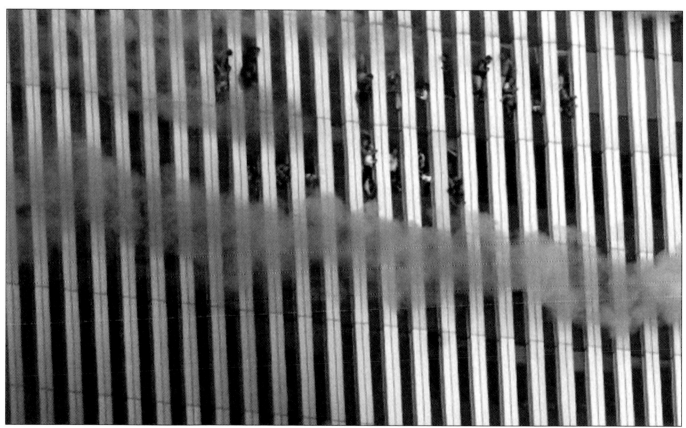

Jeff Christensen

White House Chief of Staff Andrew Card notifies U.S. President George W. Bush of the unfolding disaster. The president, who was at a reading seminar in a Sarasota, Florida, elementary school, gives a brief statement at 9:28 a.m. vowing to hunt down the perpetrators. Bush subsequently declares a global war on terrorism and launches a U.S.-led military campaign against Afghanistan for harboring bin Laden.

Win McNamee

Shocked workers emerge from the World Trade Center. Rescue workers evacuate thousands of people from the complex before the towers buckle.

Shannon Stapleton

One of the towers dissolves in a mushroom cloud of smoke, dust, and rubble.

Jeff Christensen

One of the towers plunges to the ground.

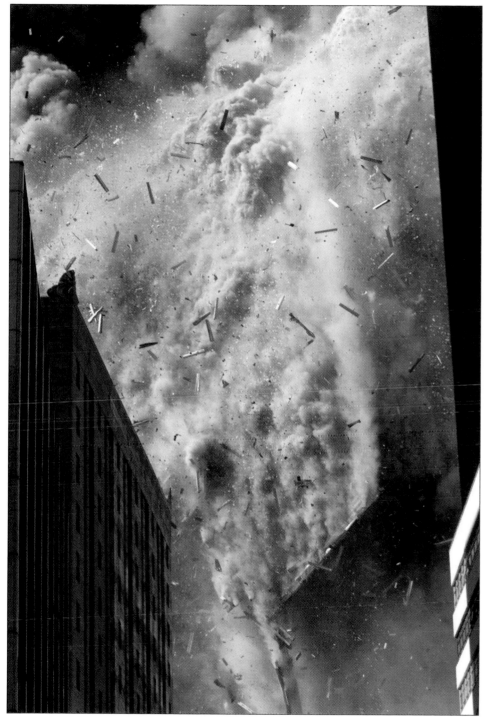

Shannon Stapleton

People flee in panic from the towering cloud of dust and debris that races up the street behind them.

Kelly Price

A man runs down Broadway to escape the choking cloud.

Kelly Price

Black smoke and dust billow through surrounding buildings as the second tower collapses at about 10:30 a.m.

Ray Stubblebine

Rescue workers remove a colleague from the wreckage of the World Trade Center.

Shannon Stapleton

A law enforcement officer expresses her anguish after the collapse of the first World Trade Center tower.

Shannon Stapleton

A dazed man carrying a briefcase and coat is caked in dust after the attacks.

Shannon Stapleton

The smoldering ruins of the World Trade Center provide a nightmarish backdrop as a man hurries past a New York subway stop.

Peter Morgan

A solitary firefighter cuts an eerie figure as he picks his way through the rubble.

Peter Morgan

The Stars and Stripes flies in the face of the devastation.

Peter Morgan

Mangled vehicles and shattered buildings in what comes to be known as "ground zero" near the base of the destroyed World Trade Center.

Peter Morgan

Firefighters carry out the harrowing task of combing the wreckage for signs of life. The rubble smolders for more than two months after the unprecedented attacks.

Peter Morgan

Firefighters are dwarfed by the scene of massive devastation.

Peter Morgan

Just outside Washington, D.C., at 9:38 a.m., barely an hour after the first New York attack, American Airlines Flight 77 slams into the southwest side of the Pentagon. A rescue helicopter surveys damage to the five-sided symbol of American military might as firefighters battle flames.

Larry Downing

The impact of the Boeing 757 on the Pentagon creates a gaping hole in the building. The attack kills 125 people in the Pentagon and 64 people aboard the plane, including five hijackers.

William Philpott

As President Bush inspects the blackened and gutted west side of the building, rescue workers on the roof of the Pentagon unfurl a U.S. flag. Workers break out into a spontaneous chorus of "God Bless America." Flags appear on cars, houses, and businesses around the country in a wave of patriotism as the nation mourns.

Kevin Lamarque

Seen here at sunrise on September 16 is the damaged area of the Pentagon with the U.S. Capitol building in the background.

Larry Downing

Accompanied by Secretary of Defense Donald Rumsfeld, President Bush, also Commander-in-Chief of the armed forces, speaks in front of the Pentagon on September 12. The president says America will not be cowed by terrorists and vows to bring those responsible to justice.

Kevin Lamarque

A U.S. Army helicopter hovers before landing in front of the damaged Pentagon on September 17.

Larry Downing

As New York and Washington reel from the attacks, United Airlines Flight 93 crashes just after 10 a.m. in rural Pennsylvania after passengers try to overpower the hijackers. Forty-four people, including four hijackers, die. Smoke rises behind investigators as they comb the field of debris near Shanksville, Pennsylvania, on September 12.

Tim Shaffer

Investigators search for the flight data recorder near a huge crater carved in the ground by the crashing plane.

Tim Shaffer

Under the watchful eye of a state trooper, travelers are evacuated from Boston's Logan airport where Flight 175, which hit the World Trade Center, originated. The U.S. Federal Aviation Administration grounds all flights departing from U.S. airports just before 10 a.m. on September 11. This is the first U.S. nationwide grounding of aircraft.

Brian Snyder

A sign flashes that all flights are cancelled from Los Angeles International Airport. The planes that hit the World Trade Center and the Pentagon were both fully laden with fuel and bound for Los Angeles. The plane that crashed in Pennsylvania was bound for San Francisco.

Jim Ruymen

As the nation grinds to a halt in reaction to the attacks, a sign over the New Jersey Turnpike in New Brunswick, New Jersey, warns travelers that bridges and tunnel crossings into New York City are closed as part of emergency security measures.

Jim Bourg

With a nation united in grief, a construction worker stands amid a patchwork of patriotic signs, American flags, and other messages hung from the scaffolding of a Times Square construction site in tribute to the victims.

Gary Hershorn

Weary firefighters leave ground zero in the early hours of September 12.

Mike Segar

New York City firefighters douse bent girders, broken concrete, and other debris at ground zero.

Mike Segar

A firefighter looks up at the remains of
the World Trade Center.

U.S. Navy Photo by Photographer's Mate 2nd Class Jim Watson

New York City firefighter John Cleary wipes soot from his face while taking a break from rescue work. Cleary helped in the rescue of two trapped Port Authority workers. Only five people were pulled alive from the rubble despite the extensive rescue effort.

Brad Rickerby

New York firefighters continue to battle blazes at ground zero on September 19.

Andrea Booher, Federal Emergency Management Agency

A firefighter calls for more rescue workers to burrow into the rubble on September 15.

U.S. Navy Photo by Journalist 1st Class Preston ¥eres

Firefighters work to dampen smoke and clear the site on
September 19.

Tom Sperduto–U.S. Coast Guard

A bird flies over the ruins of the World Trade Center as a giant American flag hangs in the background, September 19.

Kai Pfaffenbach

Firefighters are winched up in a basket after going deep under the surface at the site of the World Trade Center disaster.

Tom Sperduto–U.S. Coast Guard

Mechanical excavators methodically clear the site at ground zero, September 26.

Mike Segar

A police officer and a rescue worker look at the crushed and burned hulk of a fire truck.

Shaun Best

Workers suspended from a crane hover near what is left of the World Trade Center. Heavy excavation equipment arrives on the scene about ten days after the disaster to clear the smoldering wreckage as hope fades of finding survivors.

Kai Pfaffenbach

Smoke rises from the base of the site on September 16, five days after the attack. Some ragged sections at the base of the World Trade Center are still standing.

Shaun Best

Risking their lives in search-and-rescue
sweeps, firefighters descend deep
into the rubble, September 14.

U.S. Navy Photo by Photographer's Mate 2nd Class Jim Watson

Workers cut through steel as they clear the site. Over them, a banner expressing the feelings of New Yorkers reads, "We will never forget."

Kai Pfaffenbach

A rescue dog is transported out of the debris with pulleys and ropes in the exhaustive search for survivors, September 15.

U.S. Navy Photo by Journalist 1st Class Preston Keres

A group of rescue workers, wearing masks and goggles to protect them from the dust, leaves ground zero accompanied by two working dogs, September 29.

Jeff Christensen

Captain Robert Blume of the New York City Fire Department is hugged by his two-year-old son Brian after being promoted to battalion chief in a ceremony on September 16. One hundred and sixty-eight firefighters are promoted to replace those lost in the collapse of the World Trade Center.

Ruben Sprich

A night view of the Manhattan skyline shows the smoke and glow replacing the once distinctive outline of the landmark twin towers.

Chief Brandon Brewer–U.S. Coast Guard

President Bush's eyes fill with tears while speaking of the victims in the Oval Office on September 13. "I'm a loving guy and I'm also someone, however, who has a job to do and I intend to do it," says Bush, who also warns that America's attackers "made a terrible mistake; they have roused a mighty giant."

Kevin Lamarque

Bowing their heads in prayer, President Bush, First Lady Laura Bush, former President George Bush, his wife Barbara Bush, former President Bill Clinton, Senator Hillary Rodham Clinton, and their daughter Chelsea Clinton (left to right) attend a service at the National Cathedral in Washington, D.C., on September 14. As candlelight vigils take place across the country, Bush leads grieving Americans in prayer. "This nation is peaceful, but fierce when stirred to anger," Bush says in the service.

Kevin Lamarque

President Bush (center) talks with New York City Mayor Rudolph Giuliani (left) and New York Governor George Pataki at ground zero. As Bush tours the site on September 14 to see the devastation first hand, rescue workers cheer the president and chant, "USA! USA!" He replies, "The nation sends its love and compassion."

Win McNamee

President Bush talks to retired firefighter Bob Beckwith (right) at ground zero.
After shaking hands with weary rescuers in hard hats, Bush climbs on top of the
soot-covered remains of a fire truck and tells the throng through a bullhorn,
"I can hear you, the rest of the world hears you, and the people who knocked these
buildings down will hear all of us soon."

Win McNamee

President Bush joins Vice President Dick Cheney (left), Counselor to the President Karen Hughes, and Deputy Chief of Staff Joe Hagin (right) on the South Lawn of the White House in a moment of silence on September 18.

Larry Downing

President Bush and his wife Laura sit with two members of the military at an October 11 ceremony for the victims of the Pentagon attack, exactly one month after the plane struck.

Kevin Lamarque

Three-year-old Alana Milawski waves an American flag as she sits on her father Craig Milawski's shoulders at a candlelight vigil to honor the dead, held in Las Vegas on September 12.

Ethan Miller, *Las Vegas Sun*

Members of a church choir prepare backstage with the American flag as a backdrop during "A Prayer for America" memorial in Miami, September 18.

Colin Braley

Thousands of people gather for an impromptu memorial at the U.S. Capitol in Washington, September 12. Investigators believe the Capitol could have been a possible target of the hijacked planes.

William Philpott

A man sits in front of flowers left in tribute at the Seattle Center International Fountain on September 16.

Anthony P. Bolante

(from the left) Megan Riley, Kristen Jackson, and Elizabeth Kramer join crowds of people at the Washington candlelight vigil.

Win McNamee

A woman is overcome by emotion as she looks at posters and photographs of the missing in Union Square in New York City on September 18, one week after the attacks on the World Trade Center.

Kai Pfaffenbach

A man leans against a wall showing photographs of missing people outside Bellevue Hospital in New York on September 16.

Russell Boyce

A flower placed on a wall showing photographs of missing people outside Bellevue Hospital in New York, September 16.

Russell Boyce

A cardboard box containing a victim's shoes and a moving message becomes a makeshift shrine at New York's Union Square memorial site.

Kai Pfaffenbach

A simple note torn from a pad is laid at the Union Square memorial, along with flowers.

Jeff Christensen

A lone man looks at a wall displaying photographs of missing people outside Bellevue Hospital in New York, September 16.

Russell Boyce

People along the Hudson River waterfront in Jersey City, New Jersey, light candles for the victims of the attacks as smoke pours out of ground zero across the river, September 16.

Ray Stubblebine

A note is left next to a group of candles at a service held in New York's Washington Square Park on September 12.

Jeff Christensen

A man holds a candle and a U.S. flag at a vigil at Harrison and Greenwich Streets in lower Manhattan, just blocks from ground zero, on September 14.

Mike Segar

A man places a candle at a memorial on the sidewalk outside a firehouse in New York City in the early hours of September 14. More than 300 firefighters die in the World Trade Center attacks.

Gary Hershorn

Firefighters stand by the casket of New York Fire Department
Chaplain Rev. Mychal Judge at a funeral service at St. Francis of Assisi Church on
September 15.

Kevin Coombs

Firefighters and priests watch as the casket of New York Fire Department Chaplain Rev. Mychal Judge leaves the funeral service. Judge is eulogized as a man who ushered firefighters through life, helped the homeless, and kept vigil at the bedsides of sick children.

Kevin Coombs

Firefighters embrace outside St. Francis of Assisi Church after the service for NYFD Chaplain Rev. Mychal Judge.

Rick Wilking

Doris Gadeaille weeps on the street outside St. Francis of Assisi Church after the funeral of NYFD Chaplain Rev. Mychal Judge, September 15.

Rick Wilking

New York City Mayor Giuliani (right) watches as firefighters carry the casket of New York City Fire Department Chief Peter J. Ganci into St. Kilian Church.

Mike Segar

Mayor Giuliani bows his head as firefighters carry the casket of New York City Fire Department Chief Peter J.Ganci, a 33-year veteran of the fire department and its highest ranking uniformed officer, who died while trying to save people at ground zero.

Mike Segar

New York Port Authority police officers salute outside the Our Lady of Assumption Church in the Bronx area of New York City, September 19, at the funeral of officer Dominick Pezzulo.

Mike Segar

A woman holds a teddy bear as she cries outside a memorial service at St. Patrick's Cathedral in New York City on September 17.

Shaun Best

People mourn at a memorial mass for New York City Fire Department Assistant Chief Gerard Barbara outside St. Patrick's Cathedral in New York, October 1.

Shannon Stapleton

A fire truck containing the casket of New York City Fire Department
Chief Peter J. Ganci passes a line of firefighters on its way to his funeral on
September 15, 2001.

Mike Segar

United Airlines worker Alyson Robichaud (left) is comforted by American Eagle pilot Chuck O'Hare (right) at an interfaith prayer vigil on September 13 in Boston. The American and United flights that crashed into the World Trade Center both took off from Boston.

Brian Snyder

Peggy Ogonowski (center), wife of American Airlines pilot John Ogonowski, receives an American flag from Lieutenant Colonel James Ogonowski, the late pilot's brother, after a memorial service in Massachusetts, September 17. Ogonowski was the pilot of American Airlines Flight 11, which was hijacked and flown into the World Trade Center.

Brian Snyder

A police officer, wearing a protective mask, stands guard near the New York Stock Exchange building, which is draped with a giant American flag one day before its reopening on September 17. The four-day hiatus caused by the attacks is the longest shutdown of the New York Stock Exchange since the Great Depression.

Kevin Coombs

A New York shopkeeper vacuums dust from a store near ground zero as he tries to get back to business as usual. The entire area is blanketed with a layer of dust that rose from the site.

Shaun Best

A police officer gazes into the waters off lower Manhattan as he travels on a ferry carrying commuters from Staten Island to Manhattan on the day that the New York Stock Exchange reopens.

Ruben Sprich

In a high-profile example of heightened security, a U.S. soldier in a military vehicle patrols the financial district as people return to work prior to the opening of the New York Stock Exchange on September 17.

Dylan Martinez

As the United States tries to get back to normal, members of the New York City emergency services ring the opening bell at the New York Stock Exchange, September 17. The exchange observes a moment of silence to honor the victims of the September 11 attacks. Also in the picture are New York Senators Charles Schumer and Hillary Rodham Clinton and Governor George Pataki.

Jeff Christensen

New York Stock Exchange traders hold a "God Bless America" sign during a moment of silence to honor the victims.

Peter Jones

Jim Lawlar, a firefighter from Bridgeport, Connecticut, shoulders the American flag outside the Nasdaq market in Times Square in New York on September 17.

Kai Pfaffenbach

Commuters leaving Times Square
subway station pass posters of people
missing after the September 11 attacks.

Peter Morgan

Passersby gaze and take pictures at ground zero while returning to work in New York's financial district on September 17. Some New Yorkers wear masks because of the acrid smell around the site.

Mike Segar

New York City police officers stand close to a wanted poster printed by a New York newspaper depicting Saudi-born Osama bin Laden, named as Washington's prime suspect in the attacks.

Russell Boyce

With the return of baseball seen as another potent symbol of recovery from the attacks, players of the Colorado Rockies and the Arizona Diamondbacks hold a giant American flag prior to the resumption of major league baseball at Coors Field in Denver, September 17. Major league baseball games were cancelled after the attacks.

Gary C. Caskey

Philadelphia Phillies pitcher David Coggin (third from left) holds a U.S. flag during a memorial ceremony before the start of the Phillies versus the Atlanta Braves game in Philadelphia, September 17.

Tim Shaffer

New York Mets catcher Mike Piazza, wearing a New York City Police Department hat, waits for the start of the Mets game with the Pittsburgh Pirates in Pittsburgh, September 17. The Mets players wear baseball caps bearing the logos of the NYPD and the New York Fire Department to honor the victims.

David DeNoma

Players of the Los Angeles Dodgers and the San Diego Padres and members of the Los Angeles Police and Fire Departments stand united in the outfield of Dodger Stadium. They hold a huge American flag during a moment of silence to honor the victims on September 17.

Adrees Latif

Singer Liza Minnelli sings "New York, New York" as city firefighters and police officers clap and do a shuffle step with her during the seventh inning stretch of the New York Mets game against the Atlanta Braves at Shea Stadium in New York on September 21. This is the first baseball game to be held in New York since September 11, and many of the 35,000 fans wave American flags during emotional ceremonies that pay tribute to the victims and rescue workers.

Mike Segar

A fan waves an American flag from the upper deck at New York's Yankee Stadium as a giant version of the Stars and Stripes is unfurled in center field during a pre-game ceremony to honor the victims. The game against the Tampa Bay Devil Rays on September 25 was the first home game for the Yankees since the attacks.

Shannon Stapleton

New York City Mayor Giuliani (left) is embraced by New York Yankees' manager Joe Torre on the field at Yankee Stadium prior to the game against the Tampa Bay Devil Rays.

Mike Segar

Strangers reach across aisles to hold hands as part of the "A Prayer for America" memorial service at Yankee Stadium on September 23. Mourners in the stadium hear prayers from the world's major religions. It is broadcast on large screens in Brooklyn and Staten Island and run live on several television and radio stations.

Shaun Best

A woman holds a red rose to her forehead as she prays during the "A Prayer for America" service held at Yankee Stadium in New York on September 23.

Shaun Best

At the Yankee Stadium ceremony, Carmine Davila (left) comforts her nephew Daniel Lopez, Jr., and his sister Brittany Lopez of Brooklyn, New York, over the loss of their father, Daniel Lopez.

Jim Bourg

Frances Ortega (right) of the Bronx, New York, hugs her nine-year-old daughter Quasha and cries at Yankee Stadium. Ortega was scheduled to have a job interview at the World Trade Center on September 11 when the crash occurred, but it was rescheduled shortly before the disaster.

Jim Bourg

A police officer waves
an American flag at
Yankee Stadium.

Shaun Best

Across the Hudson River in New Jersey, a separate event for that state's victims is held in a park with views of the scarred Manhattan skyline. In this picture, a woman writes a message on a wall for victims before the start of the New Jersey Victims Memorial.

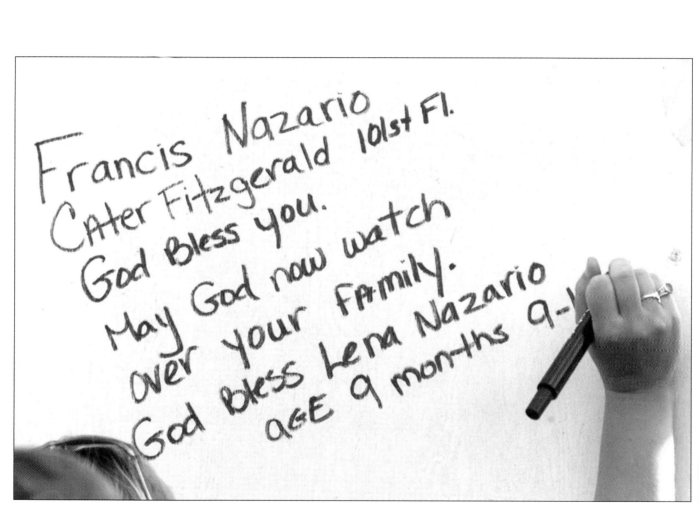

Francis Nazario
Cater Fitzgerald 101st Fl.
God Bless you.
May God now watch
over your Family.
God Bless Lena Nazario
age 9 months 9-1

Rick Wilking

With the Statue of Liberty in the background, firefighter Bill Bergner
takes part in the opening prayer at the start of the New Jersey memorial service.

Mike Segar

Britain's Queen Elizabeth leaves St. Paul's Cathedral in central London with American Ambassador William Farish on September 14.

Ferran Paredes

Britain's Prince William signs the condolence book at the American Consulate in Edinburgh for the victims of the attacks on the United States, September 21.

Jeff J. Mitchell

Win McNamee

President Bush holds up the badge of Port Authority police officer George Howard while addressing a joint session of Congress in Washington on September 20. Bush says he will carry with him the shield that belonged to Howard, killed trying to help others at the World Trade Center, and which is given to the president by the officer's mother. "This is my reminder of lives that ended and a task that does not end," says Bush. "I will not forget this wound to my country or those who inflicted it."

Shannon Stapleton

Arlene Howard waves a flag to hundreds of law enforcement representatives at the funeral of her son, George, at St. Ignatius Roman Catholic Church in Hicksville, Long Island, September 19. She sent her son's badge to President Bush.

Lisa Beamer (center), widow of Todd Beamer, as she is welcomed during an address by President Bush in the U.S. Capitol building on September 20. In the minutes before United Airlines Flight 93 went down, Todd Beamer called from a phone on board and told the air phone operator that a group of passengers was going to try to stop the hijackers. He recited the Lord's Prayer with the operator and was then heard saying, "Let's roll." A short time later the plane crashed.

Brendan McDermid

New York Governor George Pataki (right) and New York City Mayor Rudolph Giuliani (second right) clasp hands as they are applauded on Capitol Hill after Bush pays tribute to them during his address. The two men jump to their feet when Bush vows "we will rebuild New York City." First Lady Laura Bush and British Prime Minister Tony Blair (left) are also present.

Shaun Best

Senate Majority Leader Tom Daschle grips Bush in a warm bear hug following his address to a joint session of Congress in Washington on September 20. In the address, Bush says, "Our grief has turned to anger, and anger to resolution. Whether we bring our enemies to justice, or bring justice to our enemies, justice will be done."

Shaun Best

President Bush strides through the grand foyer on his way to a news conference in the East Room of the White House on October 11. Bush tells journalists the acts were "an attack on the heart and soul of the world." It is the first prime-time presidential news conference to be held since 1995.

Win McNamee

President Bush stands shoulder to shoulder with his staunchest ally, British Prime Minister Tony Blair, after a meeting at the White House on September 20.

Larry Downing

Israeli Prime Minister Ariel Sharon (right) and Foreign Minister Shimon Peres observe a moment of silence for the victims of the attacks on America at a weekly cabinet meeting in Jerusalem on September 16.

Natalie Behring-Chisholm

President Bush listens to the translation as Russian President Vladimir Putin speaks during a news conference following their meeting at the Asia Pacific Economic Cooperation (APEC) meeting in Shanghai, October 21.

Alexander Natruskin

United Nations Secretary-General Kofi Annan signs a book of condolences in the lobby of the U.N. headquarters, September 24.

Jeff Christensen

French President Jacques Chirac pauses after laying a bouquet of flowers at a memorial in Union Square in New York on September 19. The first foreign head of state to visit ground zero, Chirac praises Mayor Giuliani for his leadership, "I said from the bottom of my heart that I want to say, 'Bravo,' thank you. You did that for the New Yorkers but also for the free world, for the dignity of all the mankind, and we know that and we are beside you."

Dylan Martinez

One day after the attacks on the United States, Palestinian President Yasser Arafat donates blood for the victims in a Gaza hospital. Arafat sends his condolences to President Bush and condemns the hijackings. "We were completely shocked. It's unbelievable," says Arafat.

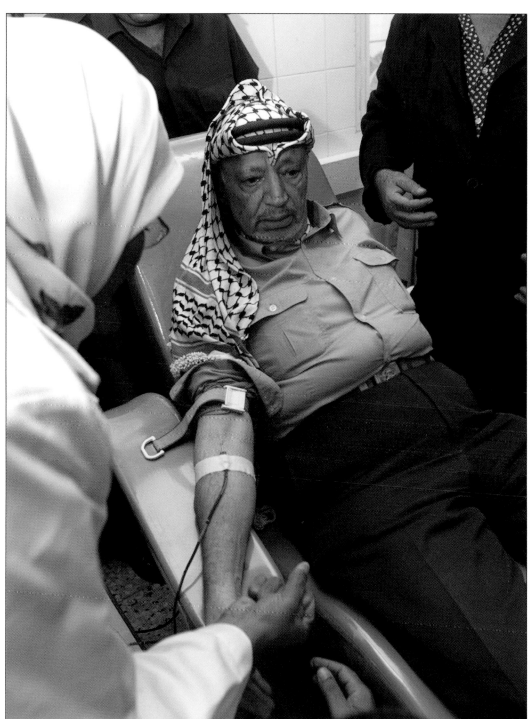

Ahmed Jadallah

President Bush and Pakistan President Perez Musharraf shake hands after a joint news conference in New York on November 10.

Larry Downing

A satellite image of Manhattan taken at 11:43 a.m. on September 12 by Space Imaging's IKONOS satellite shows a column of white dust and smoke where the World Trade Center once stood.

Spacelmaging.com

Wreckage of the World Trade Center smolders on September 15.

New York Office of Emergency Management

Aerial view of ground zero on September 26, 15 days after the attack.
Emergency workers are busy on the ground as the rubble still smolders.

The World Trade Center during the final phase of its construction in December 1970.

Slim Roomussaar

Enrique Shore

The lower Manhattan skyline is shown in an August 30 photograph, with the twin towers at center, and in a view from roughly the same site on September 27 with the towers missing.

Mike Segar

A New York City firefighter places flowers and mementos from family members of the victims amid the wreckage after a memorial service held on October 28.

Mike Segar

The Photographers

Sean Adair

was born in New York City in 1959. He was educated in New Zealand and has traveled to over 40 countries. He specializes in art, stock, and assignment freelance photography, alongside a career in video and film production. When the morning news of the first plane strike came on the television, Sean rushed up to the roof of his 20th Street, New York City apartment with his camera, telephoto lens, and tripod for a clear view of the smoking tower.

Natalie Behring-Chisholm

was born in 1972. She received her Bachelor of Arts degree in History, began her work with Reuters, Beijing, in 1997, and has since worked for Reuters in China, Israel, and the Palestinian territories. She is currently based in Jerusalem.

Shaun Best

was born in 1968 in Canada. He has been a Reuters staff photographer based in Montreal, Quebec, since February 2001. He previously worked for Reuters for six years as a contract photographer. Prior to that, he was a staff photographer at the *Winnipeg Sun*.

Jim Bourg

was born in Washington, D.C., in 1964. He started his career at the age of 16 when he began photographing for *The Washington Post*. He began shooting for UPI in 1982 before joining Reuters in 1988. He has covered a myriad of political, sporting, and general breaking-news events. He also covered the first bombing of the World Trade Center in 1993.

Russell Boyce

was born in 1962. He joined Reuters 1989 and has covered such events as the Genoa G8 summit, the Sydney Olympics, British paratroopers in Kosovo, Princess Diana, and the Gulf War.

Colin Braley

is based in Miami, Florida. He is a veteran photojournalist who continues to cover international news and sporting events throughout the U.S. and Caribbean for Reuters. His work has been published in numerous books, newspapers, and magazines throughout the world.

Gary C. Caskey

was born in 1947. He studied at the University of Michigan in Ann Arbor. From the Olympics to papal visits, Gary has numerous major event assignments to his credit. He has been a contract photographer for Reuters since 1994. A former UPI Bureau Manager, stringer for both UPI and AP, and newspaper photographer, Gary has been a photojournalist since 1975.

Jeff Christensen

was born in Duluth, Minnesota, in 1958. His first job as a photographer was for UPI in Minneapolis, Minnesota. He started working for Reuters as a contract photographer in 1989. In 1991 he moved to New York City and has been working for Reuters as a contract photographer since then.

Larry Downing

first worked as a professional photographer for a Los Angeles newspaper. He had three years of wire staff work at UPI in Washington, D.C., before spending 15 years at *Newsweek Magazine*, covering the White House. He became a staff photographer at Reuters in 1999, again covering the White House. He is currently based in Washington.

Gary Hershorn

was born in Ontario, Canada, in 1958. He worked at United Press Canada until January 1985, and it was then that Reuters hired him as Chief Photographer for Canada, in Toronto. He transferred to Washington, D.C., in 1990, where he is currently based, working as Editor, Pictures, America.

Peter Jones

was born in 1965 and is currently Chief Photographer of Reuters in Canada, based in Toronto. He has worked for Reuters since 1991.

Kevin Lamarque

has been with Reuters for the past 15 years, spending two years in Hong Kong (1987–1989) before transferring to London (1989–1999) where he covered everything from the troubles in Northern Ireland to the funeral of the Princess of Wales. He is currently based in Washington, D.C., covering the White House.

Adrees Latif

was born in Lahore, Pakistan, in 1973. He received his Bachelor of Arts degree in Journalism from the University of Houston. He has been a freelance photographer for Reuters for six years, during which time he photographed the 2000 Olympics in Sydney, The Haj (Pilgrimage to Mecca, Saudi Arabia), and the current crisis in Pakistan. An American citizen, he is now based in Los Angeles, California.

Dylan Martinez

was born in Barcelona to Argentine parents in 1969 and moved to the UK a year later. He began taking pictures for music magazines and record companies and then moved onto *Sygma* and the *Sunday Mirror*. He began freelancing for Reuters in 1991 and was made staff photographer in 1994. He worked in Asia, based in Vietnam, from 1996–1998 and is now Reuters Chief Photographer in Italy.

Brendan McDermid

was born in Buffalo, New York, in 1973. He was published for the first time in *The New York Times*, while still in high school. Brendan worked as a freelance photographer in Buffalo from 1991–1999 where he first worked for Reuters. He moved to Washington, D.C., in 1999, where he worked as a Reuters summer intern and later as a desk editor. He is now a freelance photographer based in Washington, D.C., and covers events at Capitol Hill and the White House, as well as sports and general news.

Win McNamee

was born in 1963 in Washington, D.C. He majored in journalism and graduated from the University of South Carolina in 1985. After working for newspapers for three years and freelancing for two years, he joined Reuters as a staff photographer in Washington, D.C., in 1990. McNamee has covered four U.S. presidents, three presidential campaigns, and the Persian Gulf War, as well as conflicts in the Philippines, South Korea, and Afghanistan.

Ethan Miller

was born in Austin, Texas, in 1971. He studied under Professor Frank Hoy and received a journalism degree from Arizona State University in 1994. While attending college, he worked as an intern for *The Phoenix Gazette* and *The Arizona Republic* newspapers and shot for local music magazines. Since 1995, he has been a staff photographer for the *Las Vegas Sun* and has also freelanced for Reuters, providing coverage primarily for music and boxing events.

Jeff J. Mitchell

was born in Edinburgh, Scotland, in 1970. Jeff's first full-time job in Scotland was as a photographer for the *Helensburgh Advertiser* in 1989. He then moved to the *Edinburgh Evening News* in 1992, followed by the *Herald* in 1994. It was at the *Herald* that he first worked for Reuters. Jeff has attained various prizes in the Nikon awards, the British Picture Editors Guild, and the Scottish Press Photography Awards. He is currently with Reuters in Glasgow.

Peter Morgan

was born in 1955. He received his Bachelor of Science degree in Journalism from Boston University. With the exception of a four-year stint as a staff photographer with the AP in Philadelphia (1982–1986), he worked as a freelance photographer most of his life. First in New England, then in Latin America and New York. Peter started working with Reuters as an independent contractor in New York in 1992 and was hired as Senior Photographer in New York in 1998.

Kai Pfaffenbach

was born in 1970. After studying history and journalism, he began his news photography career in Frankfurt as a freelancer for the German newspaper *Frankfurter Allgemeine Zeitung*. Kai began working for Reuters as a freelance photographer in 1996 before becoming a staff photographer in 2001. He is currently based at Reuters, Frankfurt. He has been part of the team of photographers covering the disaster that struck New York on September 11, 2001.

Kelly Price

works for JP Morgan Chase in the financial district, near the World Trade Center. She watched her office window billow like a clothes-lined sheet from the shock wave after the planes hit, and then she immediately rushed down to the street. Kelly had previously worked for a photo archive and a magazine, so was interested in documenting what was happening. "I didn't believe that I would outrun the wave [of debris] so I stopped and began shooting.... When the cloud of debris entangled me, I was relieved that I was still alive."

Brad Rickerby

was born in 1958. He received his Bachelor of Arts degree in Political Science from Reed College in Portland, Oregon, in 1980. He received his Master of Business Administration degree from Duke University in Durham, North Carolina, in 1989. Brad has worked for Reuters in New York for the past five years and has been a photographer for *Reuters World Magazine*. In addition to working for Reuters, he has shot conceptual advertising and travel stock images for Stone and the Image Bank.

Jim Ruymen

was born in 1943. He has covered the Los Angeles area for 20 years, photographing Hollywood events and awards ceremonies, such as the Oscars; sporting events, including the NBA Finals and the World Series; the criminal trials of O.J. Simpson and Charles Keating; and world news events, such as the Space Shuttle landings. He began stringing for Reuters in January 2001.

Mike Segar

was born in 1961. He received his Bachelor of Arts degree in American Studies in 1985 from Boston University and received his Masters in photojournalism in 1989 from the International Center of Photography. Mike worked as a staff photographer for the Beacon Newspapers chain in Massachusetts. He later joined the Black Star Photo Agency as an associate news picture editor. Mike joined Reuters as a contract photographer in 1991 and has since covered a full range of news, sports, political, and feature assignments throughout the U.S.

Tim Shaffer

resides in Wilmington, Delaware, where he provides photo coverage for the Philadelphia metropolitan area. He has worked 11 years as a freelancer for AP, three years on staff with Independent Newspapers Chain, has been a contributor to *The New York Times*, *The Philadelphia Inquirer*, and the *The Daily News*. He has worked as a contractor for Reuters in Philadelphia since June 1998. Since then he has participated in Reuters coverage of the Republican National Convention in 2000, as well as the 2000 NBA Finals.

Bryan Snyder

was born in 1968. He received his Bachelor of Fine Arts degree and Bachelor of Arts degree from Tufts University. He has covered various U.S. presidential campaigns, the 1994 World Cup, the death of John F. Kennedy, Jr., and the 1994 Women's Clinics shootings. He has been covering assignments for Reuters since 1989.

Ruben Sprich

was born in 1967. His main area of study was publicity photography. He began his career as photographer in Switzerland for the AP, then became a freelancer for Reuters in 1991, as well as working for various other newspapers and magazines. In 1998, he became Chief Photographer for Reuters, Switzerland, based in Zurich. Ruben has covered a variety of events in Switzerland, including the Olympics, soccer, ski, and track and field world championships.

Shannon Stapleton

was born in 1968 in Ft. Bening, Georgia. He graduated from Ohio State University in 1992 and took graduate classes in photojournalism at Ohio University. Shannon started freelancing for Reuters in March 2001. Prior to that, he freelanced in New York City. He has covered assignments including the war in Kosovo, Sierra Leone amputees, and rap artists in the Brownsville section of Brooklyn. Shannon is currently based in New York City.

Ray Stubblebine

was a staff photographer for the AP from 1971–1987, covering sports and news events. Ray was also on the crew that covered the Jonestown Massacre in Guyana, and he covered part of the "Iranscam" congressional hearings for *New York Newsday*. Since 1988, he has been a full-time contract photographer for Reuters, based in New York, where he has covered many sporting and political events.

Rick Wilking

was born in Madison, Wisconsin, in 1955. His first job as a photographer was for UPI in Denver, Colorado. He moved to Brussels in 1982 and was promoted to be UPI's Chief Photographer, Switzerland, in 1983. He joined Reuters in 1985 and was made Senior Photographer for Reuters in Washington, D.C., in 1989. Rick resigned from Reuters in 1998 and moved back to Denver where he is a freelance photographer.